Life and Basketball

Life Lessons and Basketball Tips

J OHN B ERRY

Photography, Ken Wolf from Wolf Photography (Raleigh, NC)
Hairstylist, Charles Brown from Precise Cutz & Styles (Chapel Hill, NC)
Copyediting, Darrius Jerome Gourdine from DJG Enterprises (Moncks Corner, SC)

ISBN: 978-1-4834-3054-6 (sc)
ISBN: 978-1-4834-3056-0 (hc)
ISBN: 978-1-4834-3055-3 (e)

Library of Congress Control Number: 2015906830

Lulu Publishing Services rev. date: 05/08/2015

Get a **FREE** basketball eBook that
contains plays, drills, tips, and resources
for players, coaches, and parents. Go to
the following website:

www.CoachBerry.com

For my wife, Erica,
and my two wonderful children,
Lena and Sophia

Inspiration

Geraldine Brown, my mother, is a
blessing from God. Thank you for your
lifetime of unconditional love, support,
and guidance. I owe my life to you.

Contents

Foreword

March 2015

Coach Berry is one of the most inspirational coaches I have known in my thirty years of teaching and coaching. The level of respect that the young athletes show to him when he is teaching and coaching is unmatched. This is because they know that he cares about them learning the basic fundamentals, but, more important, he wants all of the boys and girls he works with to be successful in their future endeavors.

Coach Berry is the type of coach that I want my grandkids to learn from; I strongly recommend *Life & Basketball* to anyone who loves to help young people develop into the best they can be.

Coach Ray N. Fredrick, Jr.
President & Founder
International Bouncing Bulldogs Jump Rope Team
Chapel Hill, NC

Introduction

Sports are a synopsis of life. There are many lessons to be learned about life through the playing of organized sports. There are the obvious lessons on teamwork, discipline, commitment, dedication, hard work, and so on. Then there are the subtle lessons that accompany sports, like acute attention to detail, noticing the little things, going the extra mile, and others. This book links the lessons of life with the techniques of basketball.

There are many kinds of basketball players, just as there are many different people in life. To some players, the game is nothing more than a game. There are those who see basketball as a means to stay in shape and maintain physical fitness. There are others who see basketball as a science of mental strategy among head coaches. Some see basketball as the ultimate competitive sport, as all players must be proficient in both offense and defense ... unlike football. Basketball is the one sport where you constantly confront the same defender ... unlike baseball.

If you are a student of the game, a player, a coach, or a parent, this book is for you. *Life & Basketball* provides life lessons and fundamental basketball tips in the form of short quotes.

For coaches, life lessons may be shared with the team at the start of practice. The basketball tips may be integrated within lessons plans.

For parents, life lessons may be discussed with your player. This supplements home teachings. The basketball tips enhance basketball IQ, which allows for better parent-player basketball communication.

Most of all, this book is for the player. If you love basketball; if you've ever imagined yourself as Michael Jordan, Kobe Bryant, LeBron James, or Dwayne Wade; if you think you have the jump shot of Reggie Miller, Ray Allen, or Stephen Curry; if you believe you have the handle of Chris Paul, Tony Parker, or Kyrie Irvin; or if you genuinely love the game, you need to read this book. You need to apply what is being offered in this book to your game and to your life. Think about what is being said on these pages. Live it! Play it!

Jump ball!

Note about the Book

All quotes contained within are either in regular text or *italicized* text.

The quotes that are in regular text are life lessons. The quotes in *italicized* text are basketball tips.

Also, o-player is shorthand for "offensive player."

First Quarter

Education is critical. It's the most important influence on your future quality of life. Don't shortchange yourself. Get your education.

—

The coach's number-one priority is to ensure players have a great experience, not necessarily playing time.

—

Never allow yourself to get too high or too low. Always remain even-keeled. It shows stability, maturity, and professionalism.

If your team lacks offensive skill, focus on excelling at team defense. Playing strong defense creates easier offensive opportunities.

—

No: it's a very important word. It protects you from trouble. It is used by independent, strong-minded individuals when necessary.

—

Glue guy, positive presence, fills multiple roles, willing to do whatever the team needs to succeed—coaches love these players.

Carry yourself with class. It's the right thing to do. Be an example. People are watching more than you realize.

⌒

Always be in basketball-ready position—knees bent, back straight, slight bend at the waist such that the fingertips may touch the knees. Stay ready.

⌒

It's impossible to please everyone. Someone will always be unhappy. Stick to your values and principles, communicate, and be consistent.

Emulate the janitor—first in, last out, works hard, does the dirty work, no expectation of limelight or praise. This is the ultimate team player.

—

Excuses are fictitious reasons as to why something occurred. Despise them. Never allow or use. Excuses are for losers.

—

Spend an equal amount of time on understanding why. Basketball IQ separates the contenders from the pretenders.

Don't expect others to do as you would. When you do, you set yourself up for disappointment. Instead, be pleasantly surprised if proven wrong.

—

On the best teams, players genuinely like each other and are friends. Encourage outside team-building activities.

—

Don't stutter or stammer. Always tell the truth—regardless of the consequences. A person of high character or a liar, which describes you?

To achieve a competitive advantage, significant practice time is necessary. Year-round training is a must, regardless of the sport.

—

No clowns allowed. Do the right thing—all the time. Never allow someone to influence you to participate in foolish activities. Be a leader.

—

Basketball fundamentals are critical! Magic, Bird, Jordan—they all had them. Fundamentals are the keys to success.

Be mentally tough. Things are uncomfortable. It's your move. Fight through or mail it in? For those who fight through, success will be your destination.

———

When the coach screams at a player, the player tunes out the words. When the coach whispers, the player strains to hear.

———

If your dreams don't scare you, they aren't big enough. Your teeth should be chattering. Go for it. The sky is the limit.

Common defensive failures include a lack of communication and rebounding. On ball movement, speak out. On shot, box out and secure the ball.

⁓

If you want something, start having mind-set as if you've already obtained that something. When opportunity knocks, you'll be ready.

⁓

The moment you throw in the towel, you let someone else win.

Entitlement—don't suffer from this disease. "Just because" doesn't give you the right to anything. You must earn your keep.

—

Conditional buy-in means that if players have their way (such as playing time), they're all-in, and if not, the coach is a bum. These players must be checked and asked to explore other opportunities if necessary.

—

Don't make the same mistake twice. When you do, it's no longer a mistake but a choice.

You gain confidence by gaining experience. The tougher the experience, the more confidence you'll have.

—

Critics, doubters, pessimists—they're all insignificant. All that matters is what you believe. Believe in yourself.

—

Actions speak louder than words. If a player isn't performing, don't yell and scream. Simply sit the player on the bench.

If you believe in something, believe in it all the way. It's critical to fully commit.

—

On-ball defense should be played while maintaining approximately arm's-length space from the o-player. Only close the space when the dribble is picked up.

—

For every bad situation, there is a silver lining. Look closer; you'll find something beneficial as a direct result of your experience.

Don't confuse limited playing time with your value to the team. Everybody is somebody; one player is not better than the next.

—

Always conduct yourself in an appropriate manner. You're being watched. More is being caught than taught.

—

Coaches are in the business of uplifting young men and women on and off the court. Failure to do so is a violation of their charter.

You're never too old to learn. Always seek knowledge. Remain contemporary. Be a smartphone, not a flip phone.

⌒

Cripple double is when a basketball player has double-digit points and turnovers—not good.

⌒

Experience versus observation: experience is the best teacher, yet experience may be costly; observation is almost equally great but without the negative drawbacks.

The defensive stance should be low enough such that the defender's eyes are at the chest level (of the o-player). Otherwise, the stance is too high.

⸺

It's easy to complain, "Woe is me." Take a number. Be happy with what you have while working for what you want.

⸺

When or if an o-player picks up the dribble, close out. Straddle the pivot foot. Disallow the o-player to move freely. Lock the hands together, and follow the ball.

Wrong is wrong even if everyone is doing it. Right is right even if no one is doing it. Dr. Martin Luther King Jr. said, "One person in the right is in the majority."

―

Prior to tip-off, run wind sprints. The lungs will expand. The running prevents premature tiring early in the game.

―

The commitment needed for success is vicious. Not everyone can go the distance.

See, hear, and do no wrong. Sometimes parents are unable to see a player's shortcomings. Gently and diplomatically discuss your observations.

—

Identify upfront anything worth protecting or fighting for. All other things are negotiable.

—

Value and secure the ball. Prevent unnecessary turnovers. Coaches love players who understand the importance of possessing the ball.

Not improving? Feeling stuck in a rut? Really want to reach goals? To achieve anything of significance, you must be ferociously focused.

—

An easy way to improve your game: perform five hundred control dribbles with your right and left hands every day—no exceptions!

—

Stop spending time constantly looking for more. Instead, enjoy and appreciate what you already have.

Rebounding is an underemphasized skill. It's just as important as any other skill. Don't cheat it. Work at it. Put the time in.

———

Laws of the universe are reciprocal. What you do to others will circle back and happen to you.

———

Successful teams play strong defense, rebound, break the press, and run coherent offenses against pressure defenses.

Concealing ineptness, a person can give the impression things are great. To this person, it's important to trick or fool others. Why? False pride. There is no need for this. Be appreciative and accept who you are.

———

Jab step—it's the first step that would be taken on a dribble drive. Sell it. If it's sold, opportunities are created for a dribble, pass, or shot.

———

Is someone getting under your skin? Is anger starting to set in? Relax. Take a deep breath. Don't stoop to his or her level. Show restraint. Remain focused and dignified.

Motion offense—five-out (point, two wings, and two corners), pass the ball, and cut to the basket. When the cutter reaches the rim, that player goes to the opposite corner. The next player with the ball repeats.

—

The tortoise and the hare—guess who wins the race? The tortoise. Over time, it maintains steadiness and consistency. These are life virtues worth modeling.

—

If the coach's program is solely dependent on one player, the coach doesn't have a program. It's a one-player show.

Compartmentalize your emotions. If you are angered by someone, don't take it out on the next person. That treatment is not warranted.

—

In the end, wins and losses come and go. But the effect you have on others will last a lifetime.

—

Do you want a carefree life? You understand that life is too short. Despite this mind-set, however, issues do arise. When they do, address and nip them in the bud. By doing so, you'll sleep well at night.

Shoot the ball at an angle between forty-five and fifty degrees. The ball should have a parabolic trajectory and drop into the basket (from above the rim).

—

A selfish person believes in "me, myself, and I." There is no care, consideration, or responsibility outside of self. Don't be this person. Always be mindful and look out for others.

—

Did you know that 2.5 basketballs could fit inside the cylinder of the rim simultaneously? Shoot the ball with arc. It gives the best chance for success.

Eight-track, cassette, CD, DVD, and Blu-Ray ... Technologies evolve. You must also. Constantly demand evolution, and improvement in all areas of your life.

—

In the heat of a basketball game, make the right (or simple) play, not the flashy play.

—

You're being accused of something. Instead of being defensive, listen intently. Even if accusations are 99 percent false, focus on and address the 1 percent truth. It's the most efficient way to move forward.

Informants—coaches need them in the locker room, among parents, and within the administration. They allow the coach to make adjustments to right the ship if necessary.

———

Quit? Emphatically no! At that moment, keep pushing. You're close. Quitters never win, and winners never quit.

———

Guard the yard. On-ball defense requires guarding a yard on either side of the dribbler. Outside of that yard, the help defender has time to come into play.

Driven, hard worker, goal-oriented—those are great, but be careful. Just as important is self-care. Be sure to spend quality time with family and yourself.

———

Setting ball screen—the screener approaches and performs a jump stop. The feet are shoulder-width apart. The screener's back points in the direction where the player using the screen should go. Stand strong.

———

Everyone has a unique, God-given talent. Identify yours. Add value to the community by offering your talent. Earn a fair price while at a nine-to-five. This is your side-hustle.

Develop a go-to offensive move with complementary options. You must have the ability to perform this move on both the right and left sides. Never be a one-trick pony.

———

Do you want a magic potion, a surefire way to get anything you want? How? Four letters: W-O-R-K! There are no shortcuts.

———

Fundamental offensive moves include crossover, in-and-out, between the legs, behind the back, and spin. Master these first.

Mentors are knowledge and wisdom providers. Treasure them. What? You don't have any? Read books ... lots of them. They are great substitutes.

———

Don't practice to get something right. Practice such that you can't get it wrong.

———

A person made a mistake but is in denial. This person wants to remain "perfect." Let it go! Simply utter two words: "I'm sorry." People will respect you a lot more.

Leave the refs alone. Focus on what you have control over. When your team is perfect, indulge the refs. Blaming the refs, in most cases, is straight wrong.

———

Some people make things happen. Some people watch things happen. Some people utter, "Gee, what happened?" Which one are you? Be in the first group.

———

The power dribble is an underutilized technique. To perform, turn so you are perpendicular to the defender while simultaneously dribbling with the outside hand. It protects the ball while you're under pressure.

Unconditionally love your mother, wife, and kids. Protect them at all costs.

—

The crossover dribble is most effective when the ball is released or dribbled at or below the knee level. When done correctly, it enhances the change-of-direction speed.

—

The sky is falling in. Everything has gone bad. You're in a bind. Now what? Have faith and an unequivocal belief that God is always with you. Maintain this belief through good times and bad.

Ball handling—dribbling, passing, and catching— plays a big role in coordination development. Focused effort yields competitive advantage among peers.

—

When you encounter a difficult person, who is always creating drama, what is the best approach? Give this person nothing to swing at. Be courteous and respectful. This effectively disarms that person.

—

Performed crossover dribble? Next time, hit the in-and-out move. It complements the crossover. It looks the same, except the ball is brought back to the initial side.

Perpetually knocked down? Perpetually get up! In life, no matter how many times you get knocked down, get up. Never give up!

—

At half-time, as coach, you receive the assistant's feedback. Process it. Formulate your own three observations. Address the team. Be sure to allocate time proportionately.

—

Don't buy on credit. Acquire items only after saving. Live within your means. Hate debt like it's the plague.

In any coach-parent interaction, be professional. Expectations should be transparent. The player's well-being comes first. Trust is paramount.

—

Don't ever accept being told what you can't do. Use it as gas to ignite an internal flame that is relentless. Strive until you reach your goals.

—

Your desire to score the basketball must be stronger than your defender's desire to stop you ... and vice versa. All things equal, the strongest mind wins.

In every endeavor, be the best you can be. Commit to excellence. Your driving motivation should simply be self-pride.

—

To beat the press, spread the floor, preferably full court "2-1-2" or "1-3-1". The press needs to double-team the ball. As the trap is occurring, hit the open player. This beats the press.

—

A person makes a decision, and you disagree. Now what? Beg and plead? No! Formulate your own alternative. Act on it. Always be in control of your own affairs.

Second Quarter

Step into your pass. Put your weight behind it to ensure proper velocity and control.

—

Don't rush to become famous. Pay your dues, get excellent, and then fame will come.

—

As the ball is approaching out-of-bounds, intercept it prior to it going out (even if the opponent has touched it last). The opposing team may race to secure the ball prior. This guarantees possession.

Nurturing relationships is a critical life skill, which provides personal leverage. Without them, your growth will be limited.

———

In man and zone defenses, the same principles are used. Play man defense on the strong side. Play zone defense on the weak side. Know your position relative to the ball.

———

Be a Grabowski. Pack your lunch pail. Go to work, love to work, and work all day. The next day, repeat. You must outwork the competition.

When your best player is willing to sacrifice and do things that are less glamorous, everyone else will fall in line.

———

The best indicator of future behavior is the past. If past behavior is good, continue. If not, do something to alter it.

———

Advanced skills are concatenated fundamentals. Each advanced skill may be broken down into a series of basic fundamental moves.

Never, ever physically harm a woman. By doing so, you relegate yourself to coward status! Instead, respect, protect, and cherish.

—

To rebound, do the following: box the opponent out, find the ball, and secure the ball at its highest point. Afterward, place the ball underneath your chin with elbows out, and pivot.

—

In a microwave society, we want it now with no wait time. Protect yourself against this mentality. Have the expectation that anything worth having will occur over time.

When catching, first, see the ball. Watch as it approaches. Secure it with the pads of your fingers. Do not allow the ball to touch your palms. Secure the catch. Afterward, perform the next action (such as dribble, pass, shoot, pivot, etc.).

———

Are you bored? Do you feel like your life has flat-lined? Are you stuck in a rut? Challenge yourself. Give yourself a stretch goal. Work toward it. This process has rejuvenation power.

———

In transition defense, sprint back toward the opponent's basket. While sprinting, look over your inside shoulder, talk, match up, and play defense.

Critics, everyone has them. Get used to it. Keep it moving. It's your job to hold fast to your ideals and values.

～

The role-players are the unsung heroes. Their contributions are oftentimes not praised ... yet they should be. Their presence completes the team.

～

Never accept being average. Consider that failure. Do whatever is necessary to achieve greater heights. Obsess over it.

Great on-ball defense is played with your feet. When you can dominate the o-player with your feet, you own him or her. No reaching!

⌒

What's your mind-set? Pick anything. Why not be *relentless?* Never stop until your mission is complete! Afterward, rinse and repeat. Be *relentless!*

⌒

The o-player receives a pass in the shooting area. The defender closes out. Now what? One-one-one— one fake, one dribble, and one shot. A shot fake causes the defender to jump. Dribble to the side. Shoot the ball.

Mental toughness may be strengthened as muscles are. How? Always face and find ways to overcome challenging situations.

———

No hero basketball! The player gambles in an attempt to make a big play. This gamble is off-script from what the coach asked for. If player has "apparent" success, the player is a hero; otherwise, the team suffers. Don't do it!

———

The magic of thinking big—it's liberating. Why circumstantially set boundaries on yourself? Anything is possible. Go for it!

Parent volunteers, be passionate about the team, not just your kid. The team's best interest comes first. Congrats, if this is your model!

—

Travel abroad. Do it at least once per year. Your eyes will be opened. You will obtain a better life perspective. Appreciate the daily privileges afforded in the United States.

—

Fire in the belly, some players have it; some don't. For players who have it, it's easier to tone down (if necessary). For players who don't, it's hard to kick-start, even if you want to.

Procrastination? No movement toward goals? What's the escape plan? Do what you're supposed to do ... *now*! What are you waiting for?

—

The team is not playing cohesively and is making inexcusable mistakes. Gong show! This is not good. Encourage the team to tighten up. Team self-accountability is a must. Demand it.

—

Fear represents a growth opportunity. Stand up to it. Each time you do, you gain strength, confidence, and courage.

The ball comes off the backboard or rim. Don't wait. Go get it. Jump. Secure the ball at its highest point. Whoever wants it the most is likely to win.

I don't have this. I don't have that. Be grateful for what you have today. Work hard for what you want tomorrow.

A time-out is called. Why? Address inefficiencies. Rest players, and insert substitutes. Players who are in the game will sit. Players who are not will stand in a semi-circle. Whatever the issues, make the necessary adjustments.

If you have a strained family relationship, it doesn't matter if it's the other person's fault; initiate reconciliation, not for them, but for you. It's stress liberating.

—

B.E.E.F., balance, eyes, elbow, follow-through—shot correctness and mechanics are more important than shot conversion.

—

Be goal-oriented. Review goals (at least) twice daily, when you wake up and before you go to sleep. This forces you to focus on achieving them.

ROBOT shot principles—know your (R)ange, get (O)pen, be (B)alanced, catch and shoot in (O)ne motion, and ensure no (T)eammate has a better shot than you do.

———

Don't judge a book by its cover. Everyone you meet has something to offer: knowledge, wisdom, and experience. As a bonus, you'll learn what not to do.

———

Triple threat—stand with feet shoulder-width apart, knees bent, and back sloped, so the nose is even with the knees. Afterward, place the ball on the hip (right or left sides), with the strong-side hand on top of the ball and the weak-side hand on the side.

Everyone has a gift. It is something you're the best at with the least amount of effort. It's instilled in you. Identify your gift.

—

Boxing out—engage the man, pivot, and seal. Afterward, find the basketball and secure it at its highest point (if possible).

—

If facing a bully, avoid the fight at all costs. If you are physically attacked, defend yourself. You have the right to do so.

Secondary defensive play is critical. It's when the second defensive player comes over to help. You must have it, or your defense will be rendered useless.

———

When lacking something, give it. After giving, you'll receive that which you gave. The law of giving and receiving works hand in hand.

———

When passing the ball to a teammate, do something: cut to the basket, set a screen, or reposition to an alternate court location.

True success goes out to those who sacrifice. This is necessary in education, relationships with family and friends, health, and work. Life is all about sacrifices.

———

When playing defense, stay between your opponent and the basket. At the same time, watch the ball. The ball is your primary responsibility. Your opponent is second.

———

Do you desire to achieve a specific milestone but don't have a road map? Yes. Now what? Get a mentor. Mentors take you from where you are to where you want to go.

Dribbling, passing, and shooting all require the same mechanics: the extension of the arm while locking the elbow and snapping the wrist.

———

Stop blaming others for your personal failures. The blame game is simply an excuse to remain mediocre.

———

If the coach is pushing you, he or she likes you. If the coach is ignoring you, start getting worried.

Drama is a frivolous situation that should never happen. It's the antithesis of solitude. Pride yourself on avoiding drama.

—

Sport, if coached properly, is a microcosm of life. There are ups, downs, teamwork, getting up when feeling down, overcoming fears, and so on.

—

Be careful what you ask for. Oftentimes, it's not all that you thought it would be. Appreciate what you have.

Technique is needed to play defense. Just as important are desire and determination. These traits will enhance defensive skills.

—

Good versus evil, right versus wrong—at decision time, what will you do? Hopefully, you'll do the right thing. Listen to your inner voice.

—

Coaching, do it because it's part of your soul. Live to help and inspire others to achieve something that couldn't be done alone.

Nothing comes to a sleeper but a dream. It is great to have big dreams, but equally important is having a plan and executing it.

~

The post player backs down the defender. The defender is losing the battle. As such, the defender steps to the side, "pulls the chair." The post player falls. A travel violation is called.

~

Don't focus on the destination; instead, enjoy the journey.

As you are closing out on the o-player, a shot fake is given. Don't go for it! Keep your feet. Only when the o-player leaves his or her feet should you contest the shot.

———

Talkers are a dime a dozen. Action takers are few and far between.

———

Stay away from the coffin corner. The coffin corner is the area of the basketball court (at the baseline or half-court corners), where the defense can easily apply a trap.

A sailor never became skilled in smooth waters. Expect rough seas. Through it all, you'll be better.

———

If your kid explores many sports, identify the sport where he or she has the most interest. Feed the beast! Set up and allow the kid to engage that sport as much as possible.

———

The hustle—it's the relentless pursuit of a goal. This person doesn't mind taking the stairs, as opposed to the elevator. What matters is he or she *must* get the job done!

The o-player picks the dribble up prematurely, and the defender closes. Now what? Be ball strong. Pivot back and forth through the defender's legs. Buy time. Pass the ball.

———

Don't be a jack-of-all-trades but master of none. Select a trade you're passionate about. Afterward, focus on being great at that trade.

———

Armchair quarterbacks are running rampant. Let's keep things simple. Stay in your lane. Players play, coaches coach, referees ref, and parents cheer.

Want something? Develop a plan. Execute. No matter what, keep working it. Discipline gets you from point A to point B.

—

Great teams work together. Members know their roles. As a result, big things are possible. Teamwork makes the dream work.

—

Peer pressure? At decision time, fall back on your morals and principles. Use them as a guide. No deviation.

Ball-screen offense: The screener's defender is the key player. There are three options available to the dribbler: "dribble-drive layup", "in-between jump shot", or "pocket pass to the roller/popper."

———

Who are you? Identify your three closest friends or associates. It's a great mirror.

———

Ball-screen defense: The screener's defender is the key player. There are three options available to the screener's defender: "sag", "switch", or "hedge."

You don't have to get along with everybody, but you must be able to work with anybody.

—

"Hard work on three. Hard work on three. One, two, three, hard work!" Hard work beats talent when talent won't work.

—

For any given situation, always know your objective. Assess what is being presented. If the presentation is in-line with your overall objective, move forward. If not, explore other options.

Shot fake—Was only a head bob given? If yes, this is a common mistake. Three things are needed when shot faking: rise on the balls of the feet, initiate the shot motion (by showing elbows), and yes, bob the head.

You're in pursuit of a goal, head down, forging forward. Periodically, stop, look up, and smell the roses. Afterward, get back to work.

You just received a pass for an open shot. Your shot was initiated "after" the catch. Too slow! Your shot is now being challenged. An effective scorer must be able to catch and shoot in one motion.

Something happened. You're not too thrilled. You want to lash out verbally. It's better to wait (and think about it) than to act prematurely.

———

Attacking zone defenses include dribble-drive the seams, initiate ball reversals, flash the middle, play behind the zone, and screen the zone.

———

Be a person of your word. Do what you say, and say what you mean.

Great drills are multifaceted and include: skill development, set breakdown (offense/defense), and conditioning.

———

Don't take a person's kindness as a weakness. Oftentimes, the kind person is the one to worry about.

———

A great youth workout includes fifty push-ups, fifty sit-ups, and fifty air squats every day.

An effective argument approach is to ask loads of questions. The questions will force the other person to reevaluate his or her reasoning. You could also avoid the argument altogether.

———

A kid falls down and gets hurt. Short-term, that's not good. Long-term, it's great! It serves to toughen the kid mentally and physically.

———

Comparing yourself to someone else is a big mistake. You have no control over this other person. Simply be the best "you" that "you" can be.

Always catch the basketball with two eyes, two hands, and two feet (while stepping toward the ball).

———

What is the difference between a tell-me and a show-me person? The tell-me person talks a good game, but does nothing. The show-me person talks very little, but is all about action. Be the latter.

———

The o-player dribble drives. The help defender rotates to take the charge. The defender has his or her feet set that are shoulder-width apart, knees are bent and arms are out. Now what? "Scrape the plate." Take the full charge.

The only time you run out of chances is when you stop taking them.

—

Free throw: Align the strong foot with the middle of the basket. The feet should be shoulder-width apart and slightly staggered. Initiate the dribble routine. See the basket. Shoot the ball (while the shooting elbow is tucked in).

—

Initiate a random act of kindness. Help a homeless person. Hold the door open for an elderly person. Compliment someone, and so on. Try it sometime.

Sport and personal character—sport character is important for game performance; more important, personal character is critical for life.

Stop trying to impress others who don't care about or think of you. Simply impress the person in the mirror.

Plays are not effective. Nothing seems to work. Think again. Oftentimes, it's not about the X's and O's. It's about the Jims and Joes. You simply must play harder and smarter!

You're a product of your environment. Assess the product. Make changes, if necessary.

———

Sport participation is no longer seasonal. High-performance athletes train year-round. It's the new normal.

———

Follow your heart and passion, but have a plan. The two together will likely yield success.

Third Quarter

Are you defeating yourself? Perhaps you're experiencing lapses in concentration. You must focus and limit the distractions; this maximizes your chances of success.

———

Success is the result of becoming the best you can be with what's been given to you.

———

Helicopter parents, no hovering. Oftentimes, it does more harm than good. Let go. Allow your kid to grow freely, without being overbearing.

When building relationships, you must invest a great deal of time. The more time invested, the stronger the relationship.

~

You don't win with the five best players. You win with the five players who play best together.

~

Never cross the person who has helped you. It shows no appreciation and is disrespectful. This person then would be less likely to help you again.

Postgame Speech
If you won the game, lavish the praise but point out areas needing improvement. If you lost the game, be careful. Be easy and soft on critiques.

———

You're going to take the world by storm. No one has ever seen what's about to happen. Great! Don't talk about it; be about it.

———

Work just as hard to be a great teammate as you do at becoming a great player.

When you talk, you're repeating what you already know. If you listen, you may learn something new.

———

Every player must sacrifice a little of him- or herself for the good of the team. This is critical for team success.

———

Pleasing everyone is impossible. Stick to your principles. You'll be able to look in the mirror knowing you did what you thought was right.

Dependability is more important than ability. Be there; show up every single time.

—

Trust—it's very hard to find but very easy to lose.

—

In-game competition is combat. Expect the worst. Overly physical play, refs cheating ... so what! Tighten your shoelaces, and fight on!

If you lend money, do so without the expectation of getting it back.

Coaching 101
If the team loses, be in the foreground, and accept responsibility. If the team wins, be in background and give praise to others.

Credibility is everything. Practice what you preach. Otherwise, your words will hold less substance.

Only 0.03 percent of high school basketball players get drafted into the NBA. As a backup, get your education. Education is the only sure thing you can depend on.

~

Give others respect by hearing them out. It's your job to separate the wheat from the chaff. If the information is valuable, keep it. If it is not valuable, chuck it.

~

Keep your priorities in order: God, family, education, and then your sport of interest.

Don't ever take anything for granted. Live every day to the fullest. You never know what may happen. Tell your loved ones you love them daily!

⁓

Coaches build champions, not necessarily in the field of play, but in life.

⁓

Presumptions and Profiling
Based on prior experiences, your lens may be blurred. Therefore, observe, be open, and ask questions. Afterward, conclude.

Coaches love players who are willing to do what's best for the team and have the capacity to fill multiple roles. Be that player who offers value.

―

Feeling stressed? Overwhelmed? Take a long shower. It has a soothing effect. Your thoughts are crystallized so new ideas and approaches surface.

―

Communication etiquette: admonish in private, reward in public.

Being cocky is bad. Being confident is great! Why? Cockiness exemplifies conceit. Confidence exemplifies assurance. They're polar opposites.

—

The coach's responsibilities include skill development, team development, sportsmanship, life lessons, and fun.

—

Presentation, exam, job interview—there is some pending significant event. You're worried. Remember this: 80 percent of life is showing up, and 20 percent is the actual task.

Coaches must let players know that they care for them and can be trusted.

Whenever you commit to something, do it. An old adage is "underpromise and overdeliver."

Don't allow a few bad apples to ruin things for the rest of the team.

The essence of life is to identify and care for something bigger than yourself. Leave a legacy.

―

During practice, players should take game-like shots from comfort spots on the floor.

―

Ultimate job-security is found in maintaining the requisite marketplace skill set. Update when necessary. This allows a person to stay in high demand.

Younger players (five to eight years old) may shoot the ball by placing each hand (right and left) on each side of the ball, if necessary. Be sure their shoulders and feet are square to the basket.

⁓

Nervousness is a natural human emotion. When experiencing it, take deep breaths (with your eyes shut). On the exhale, count to ten. Repeat until you are settled.

⁓

Three-point rules were brought to the game in 1984. For high school, the three-point line distance is nineteen feet, nine inches.

It's easy to want something. It's very hard to commit and follow through to make it happen. Persevere until completion.

—

From the start, the coach should teach equal hand development. This ensures that the player can proficiently dribble with either hand.

—

God doesn't make mistakes. Based off past actions and decisions you've made, you're exactly where you're supposed to be. Accept it. Move on.

When you are dribbling, use angles, protect the ball, avoid pressure, keep your head up, and move with a purpose.

———

Focus on one thing at a time. The most important thing at any given moment is the immediate task; nothing else matters.

———

Don't stop dribbling until you know the next action. Picking the ball up prematurely invites the defender to close out and pressure the ball.

Memories are life treasures. Spending time with kids, hanging out with friends, and reminiscing about experiences growing up create memories. Cherish them.

———

When making a basketball move, the player should visualize dribbling under a shelf. This forces the player to stay low.

———

Set high expectations for yourself. Be your hardest critic. Prove your worthiness to yourself, not to others.

Steady, relentless pressure over the entire game harasses and tires the opponent.

—

Friends are plentiful when you're successful but scarce when times are tough. Identify real friends who are willing to be in the foxhole with you during trying times.

—

Pressure defense results in bad passes, deflections, and turnovers.

Being confronted? Listen without being defensive. Now, it's your turn. Speak without offending.

⌒

Good pressure defense is not a gambling defense; it's a defense that extends pressure all over the floor.

⌒

Identify your calling. You'll notice its gravitational pull. Don't fight it; go with the flow. You are destined for such a thing.

Do your job. Trust others. If everyone does his or her job, guess who benefits. The team. Play for the name on the front of the jersey, instead of the one on the back.

———

Life isn't fair. The truth is most things that happen to you, others have already experienced. Learn to overcome. Have no built-in excuses.

———

A surefire way to determine a coach's expertise is to view and evaluate practice sessions.

If you're going to do something, go all out. There is no in-between. Why settle for mediocrity? That's failure. Get the whole enchilada!

———

Losses are inevitable. You may lose the game, but don't beat yourself up. Instead, learn from it.

———

What's the difference between cowardly and courageous? Cowardly runs and hides under the table. Courageous confronts and stands up to its fears.

Good offense attacks the weakness of the defense. Good defense attacks the strength of the offense.

—

Everyone comes from somewhere. Appreciate your upbringing. Respect others. No one's town or situation is better, only different.

—

Practice sessions should include the following elements: instruction, skill development, basketball IQ, conditioning, and competition.

Cliques? Don't like them. They tend to be standoffish. They make others feel unwelcome. Avoid being a part of cliques. Open yourself up, and be friendly to others.

—

Great coaches teach players what they need to know; not everything they personally know.

—

Periodically, take time to say thanks to those who've helped you. The recipient feels appreciated. It exemplifies class and gratitude.

High school teams averaging eight-plus steals per game win 69 percent of their games.

— ⁓ —

In any given situation, expect and prepare for the worst. Never get caught off-guard. If all is well, there will be nothing to address. If not, you'll be prepared.

— ⁓ —

Talent is naturally acquired. Skill is developed over time (often years) by drilling and practicing.

Enjoy the present. Cherish your blessings. Live life to the fullest. Nothing is guaranteed.

———

Coaches should always tell players (and parents) the truth ... even if it hurts.

———

Starting and finishing something is exciting! Sustaining throughout is very tough. To do so, mental perseverance and toughness will be required.

Parents have the collective power to build up or tear down a program. Parents are critical to success. Involve and value them.

———

Success requirement: Make being successful your top priority. Eat, drink, and sleep it. Have the mind-set that it's life or death. Once you do this, you'll succeed.

———

Parents should not live their lives through their kids. Instead, they should be supportive and encouraging.

Feeling down? Want to throw in the towel? Snap out of it! No one feels sorry for you. Look up, stand up, and never give up!

———

A player's skill, talent, attitude, and work ethic determine his or her playing time. If you are not playing much, reassess the items noted above.

———

It's a foregone conclusion that things are going to happen. Accept this. What are you going to do about it? Your action will determine your medal.

At each practice, players should have the mind-set of getting 1 percent better. This requires a clear and concise focus.

——

Your approach to anything is an indication of how you'll approach everything.

——

Big-shot Bob, Robert Horry, is an all-time great clutch shooter who was always ready. Think, prepare, and drill for that moment. Be ready when you are called on.

The decisions you make today will have lasting implications tomorrow, positive and negative.

—

Focus on the next play. Nothing can be done about the past. Move on. All energies should be concentrated on what's ahead.

—

Every day, you make choices. Sometimes, a choice will select you. At that moment, stand strong. Serve as an excellent example to follow.

In real estate, it's location, location, and location. In coaching, it's communication, communication, and communication (especially if you're losing).

———

Don't allow just anyone entrance in to your inner circle. Trust must be earned over time. Allowing the wrong person in could prove costly.

———

Team creed: accomplishments are boundless when no one cares who gets the credit.

Real leaders lead by example, not by telling others what to do.

⁓

What is a good game shot? The player should have an 80 percent shot conversion rate when unguarded (in practice, at game speed). If this criterion is met, shoot the ball. Otherwise, pass.

⁓

Be willing to go where others won't. Doing so allows you to achieve what others don't.

About postgame parental communication—don't do it. It's the worst time to talk, especially after a loss. Instead, wait until emotions are quelled. This usually happens by the next day.

—

You've made mistakes. Stop killing yourself! Apologize if necessary. Learn, grow, and move on from them.

—

Sacrifice, it's the cornerstone of every great team. All team members should do what's best for the team.

Forgiveness is powerful. Forgiving renders the instigator powerless.

~

Aimed versus natural shots: Aimed shots are overthought and shot to be perfect. Natural shots are taken subconsciously; the shooter simply lets the shot fly. Natural shots are better.

~

The accumulation of more responsibility means facing more unforeseen challenges. Mentally, you must remain sharp.

Prior to passing the ball to a teammate, ensure the teammate will not be in a compromised position where a turnover is likely.

—

Everything in your soul is telling you to abandon the mission. You must fight against this and finish what you started.

—

Statistics show that shot accuracy decreases 12 percentage points when shots are contested.

Fourth Quarter

Respectful dialogue and a friendly demeanor are very effective against a rugged, tough person. This forces the person to respond in a like manner.

———

Three, the hard way—it's a traditional three-point play. The player scores a two-point basket and is fouled. Thereafter, the player makes a free throw.

———

Oftentimes, the quietest person has the most active mind.

Big-Game James
James Worthy is a Laker legend. He had a reputation of playing huge in big games. When the lights come on, you've got to perform.

~

Treat others the way you'd like to be treated.

~

Defensive concepts include a strong side, a weak side, boxing out, stances, slides, and so on. There is a lot to understand in order to play intelligent defense.

Loyalty is a critical character trait. It shows graciousness to those who are in your corner. Be sure to give homage to those who deserve it.

———

You have absolute control over effort and attitude. These alone can propel you to great achievements.

———

All you can do is be the best you can be. Doing this makes you a success.

Although winning and losing aren't everything, they carry great weight regarding a person's emotional psyche. It's jubilation or misery. Know and keep this in mind.

———

Mistakes are part of the growth process. Don't get discouraged. Each mistake represents one step closer to the intended outcome.

———

All decisions made should be in the best interest of the team. Coaches should never sacrifice team integrity for an individual.

Revenge is a negative intent and should be avoided, as it shows tremendous immaturity. Instead, be sure your intentions are for the good.

———

Desire, heart, and hustle—these are key ingredients to successful defensive play.

———

Always confront your fears. Don't run from them. If you do, you'll have to live with that fact. This is far worse.

Being a champion is a mind-set. Perform your best in every endeavor you're involved in, even if you're not up to it.

⌒

Being nice to someone you dislike doesn't mean you're fake. It demonstrates great maturity, which allows toleration of this person.

⌒

When dealing with an irrational parent, the coach must understand. Be the piñata. Take the hits. Be an example by responding in a professional manner.

Love is the most profound and life-altering treasure a person could have. Seek and obtain it, even if it takes a lifetime.

⁓

It is a team voyage. Players are aboard a ship. Each player is a cog in the wheel, which allows the mission to be accomplished. There is no room for selfishness. It's all about the team.

⁓

You're the CEO of *You, Inc.* You decide what, why, and how you're involved in anything. This includes a job, a side-hustle, a volunteer opportunity, or a hobby. Be in control.

Player-coach communication is a must. It ensures everyone is on the same page regarding role, playing time, and expectations.

—

Expect things to happen. Some things will not be favorable. At that point, improvise, adapt, and overcome.

—

Unless a team is supertalented offensively, defense will be the key to success. Focus on and demand it.

When you stop having external problems, it's an indication that you don't have enough responsibility or you're not seen as important.

———

Significant individual improvement happens by practicing on your own. Team improvement happens during practice.

———

Each time you engage someone, give something: a smile, a compliment, and/or positive energy.

During play, great players do what's best for the team at any given moment.

⸻

Childhood memories of parents, neighborhoods, old friends, schools attended, and so on allow you to use the past to ensure the next generation benefits.

⸻

If you cannot shoot a left-handed layup comfortably, perform a jump stop and shoot the ball as a jump set shot. As a priority, develop your left hand to alleviate this issue.

A successful life begins and ends with God.

———

Coaches hate when the ball sticks. Dribbling is about me; *passing is about* we. *Move the ball. Allow the offense to flow.*

———

No one cares what you did yesterday. All that matters is what you'll do today.

When it comes to choosing between an average but consistent player and a very good but sporadic player, many coaches prefer the average player. From the coach's vantage point, he or she knows what to expect every single time and can prepare accordingly.

———

Self-discipline—every day, do what you're supposed to do regardless of how you're feeling.

———

A great teammate steps in and takes the heat for another teammate.

Continue to be nice to others even if one bad apple takes advantage. It's a reflection on the bad apple, not on you.

———

For a competitive edge, players must improve their skills year-round. Otherwise, it's unrealistic to believe anything significant will be accomplished.

———

It's okay to forgive. Move beyond the offender's shortcomings, but don't put yourself in a position where the same thing can happen again.

Being a team leader is an acquired skill. How do you acquire it? Study successful teams, understand the coach's philosophy, and serve others.

———

Be generous with your compliments while being stingy with your condemnation.

———

Team captains aren't necessarily team leaders. Team leaders are the ones who control the locker room.

Study in thirty- to fifty-minute bursts. It maximizes your retention rate. In between, take ten-minute breaks.

———

Offensive Rebounding
When a defender turns his or her head, slash in a direct line to the basket. Go around the defender if necessary.

———

Assume anything said about someone will get back to that person. Be complimentary, or don't say anything at all.

Defensive Rebounding
Figuratively, throw the first punch. Initiate contact with the o-player: forearm in chest, pivot, seal, hunt for the ball, and secure the rebound.

—

Great leaders are also great followers. In order to lead, you must learn to follow first. This is how leadership is learned.

—

Offensively limited? Need more scoring? How? Limit the opponent to one shot, secure offensive and defensive rebounds, secure steals, and block shots.

Don't contribute to the wealth buried in graveyards. Many have moved on to the next life without realizing their potential. Go for it!

———

Shooting drills should mirror offensive sets—versus man and zone defenses.

———

With regard to sibling rivalry, battle and compete within a private setting; once in public, compete against others and have each other's back. Blood is thicker than water.

On the court, if you have to think about it, it's too late. Sets, tactics, and plays must be committed to muscle memory. Otherwise, you're behind.

———

Avoid fighting at all costs. Sometimes, you can't. Be prepared. Over 90 percent of street fights end up on the ground. As a form of self-defense, consider embracing Brazilian or Gracie Jiu-Jitsu.

———

Each year, a challenging off-court event will threaten the well-being of a team. Maintain your professionalism. As coach, be fair but firm. Address the situation appropriately.

Always believe. Others will take a chance on you if you're willing to take a chance on yourself.

———

All you can control is yourself, not the opponent. Your preparation and game performance will have a heavy hand in determining the outcome.

———

Procrastination is the order of the day. Nothing is getting done. Snap out of it! It's time to get serious about being serious.

A great team should be able to function during games with minimum direction from the coach.

——

If you have an issue with someone, gently approach him or her to converse. Don't talk behind his or her back. The worst thing you can do is smile in a person's face but stab him or her in the back.

——

Regardless of the system being run, without skilled players, it won't work.

What you see depends mainly on what you're looking for.

———

Unless a player wants to join his or her parents (during a game), he or she should stop looking in the stands for comfort and guidance.

———

Don't listen with the intent to reply. Listen with intent to understand.

Play a system suited to the team's abilities and one that the coach has mastered. Mastery allows for easy adjustments based on an opponent's tendencies.

———

Keep God inside, and be the best you can be.

———

Good offense forces the defense to move north, south, east, and west by initiating multiple ball reversals. If done, the defense is more likely to make mistakes.

Sometimes, it's best to mind your own business. Simply say, "My name is Bennett, and I ain't in it!"

⌇

Secondary Break
Both wings are filled, and there is a rim runner. The guard advances or pushes the ball to the first available option for a transition basket. If nothing is there, seamlessly flow into an offensive set.

⌇

Perception unchallenged becomes reality.

On your team, be open to suggested roles and responsibilities. Your versatility determines your usability.

———

Always respect your elders even if you dislike or disagree with them.

———

Just because you got benched doesn't mean the game is over. Continue to work as if you're the starter. When another opportunity knocks, you'll be ready.

If you're a principle-based person, most decisions are already made prior to any encounter.

⌒

Winning and losing, oftentimes, is the sole barometer for validation. Don't allow it to be. Objectively evaluate the total picture, and then conclude.

⌒

You must keep your cool when being tested. Otherwise, you're allowing an unworthy person to control you.

Great rebounders don't go after rebounds with one hand; they go after them with two.

———

Stress, anxiety, tension—Why? Only worry about those things that you can change or do something about.

———

No one can accomplish great things on his or her own; it takes a team.

When going through adversity, get on your knees, pray to God, and surround yourself with loved ones.

———

Don't be afraid of taking chances and failing. With great risk comes great reward.

———

The only difference between criticism and feedback is how you hear it.

Players fall into one of three groups: skilled players, role players, and developing players. Developing players should take the long view and understand they are the future. Their playing time, most likely, will be limited.

—

Everyone around you is panicking. It would be very easy to join in. Resist this. No matter what, always keep your cool and remain calm. Assess the situation, and act accordingly.

—

During practice, shoot shots likely to be available during games: free throw, elbow, short corner, and so on. Don't waste your time shooting unlikely shots.

A person doesn't change. Regardless of life experiences and accomplishments, the core of a person is still the same.

———

When the o-player dribble drives and blows by the defender, the defender may attempt to swat the ball away from behind. To avoid this, the o-player should perform a "quick" crossover dribble and back as soon as the blow-by occurs.

———

Your level of success will be determined by how well you embrace and manage pressure.

Play your game. Understand your strengths and weaknesses. Do the things you do well. This is especially useful during tryouts and game play.

———

Don't overthink anything. No analysis paralyses. Instead, make a decision and move on. Adjust as needed. It's called "fire, aim, ready."

———

Don't let the smooth taste fool you! A well-mannered player off the court may very well be a ferocious, highly competitive player on the court.

Serve only one master. Don't stretch yourself too thin by engaging too many projects. You'll never reach your potential on anything. Instead, focus in on one thing and become great at that!

As the coach, put players in positions that accentuate their talents. Don't force players into a system. Make the system adjust to the players.

If something isn't working, try something different! Don't be stuck in your ways. Insanity is doing the same thing repeatedly but expecting different results.

Successful coaches have at least one player who is a great leader on and off the court. This player gets others to buy in to what's being preached by the coach.

———

It is far more important to be known as a great person than as a great athlete.

———

Limited playing time? Cut from the team? There's nothing stopping you from conducting your own practice sessions. In fact, it's a must in order to address your inefficiencies.

You're traveling down the wrong road—making bad decisions, being irresponsible, being lazy. It's never too late to make a U-turn.

———

Outside of X's and O's, the biggest and most important characteristic of an assistant coach is loyalty.

———

Should've, would've, could've—terrible! Don't be more disappointed by the things you didn't do than the things you did do.

Early morning practices are proven to increase mental focus and acuity for up to ten hours postpractice—hence, better school production.

Change something by changing it. How? Put together a plan. Stick to it until the change is secured.

Play a practice game without dribbling. In this game, no one is allowed to dribble. It will force everyone to focus on passing.

About the Author

Coach John Berry has been coaching basketball since 1993. He has worked with over two thousand kids and coached over one thousand games. Coach Berry has coached at the recreational, travel, AAU, junior varsity, and varsity levels and is now varsity head coach at Woods Charter High School (Chapel Hill, North Carolina).

Coach Berry's love for basketball began at an early age in North Philadelphia, Pennsylvania. As he was growing up, sports were everything to him. Every day, Coach Berry would go to the playground and play against or with childhood friends. In the summer months, Coach Berry would watch relatives play in organized street leagues in front of large crowds. Coach Berry was a ferocious fan of the Philadelphia 76ers, led by the great Julius Erving. Among relatives and friends, debates were held, strategies consummated, and tons of film studied.

Throughout high school, Coach Berry was very undersized. As a freshman, he was four feet, ten inches tall, weighing sixty pounds! As a senior, he was five feet, four inches tall, weighing eighty pounds! Given the makeup and strength of his high school varsity basketball team (Murrell Dobbins Area Vocational Technical School, Philadelphia, Pennsylvania), he knew it would be very difficult to secure a spot. In fact, that team was ranked number one in the United States in 1985! Eventually, that team would produce three NBA players: Hank Gathers (RIP), Bo Kimble, and Doug Overton.

Instead, Coach Berry studied the game as a coach. He would attend every home basketball game, converse with coaches and varsity players, and watch as many local high school, college, and NBA games as possible. Over time, Coach Berry developed that coach's edge.

As founder and lead skills development coach for YouthHoops.com (since 2008), Coach Berry runs year-round basketball camps, which emphasize fundamental skill development, basketball IQ, and life lessons.

Coach Berry has a bachelor's degree from Howard University (1990) and a master's degree from Temple University (1992). He is a member of Alpha Phi Alpha Fraternity Incorporated, Beta Chapter. In addition, Coach Berry is a Gracie Jiu-Jitsu practitioner under the leadership of Royce Gracie black belt, Mazi Heydary (Chapel Hill Gracie Jiu-Jitsu).

During Coach Berry's coaching tenure, he has always infused life lessons, character enrichment philosophies, and a surgical style of instruction into his programs. These very things, for the first time, are being shared in this book, *Life & Basketball*.

Coach Berry is married to Erica Berry and has two lovely daughters, Lena and Sophia. Currently, Coach Berry and his family reside in Chapel Hill, North Carolina.

Get a **FREE** basketball eBook that
contains plays, drills, tips, and resources
for players, coaches, and parents. Go to
the following website:

www.CoachBerry.com

Skill Development Basketball Camps

Ages: 6–14 (boys and girls)

www.YouthHoops.com
@RealYouthHoops

+1-919-533-5919

Licensing Opportunities Available
(USA & Worldwide)

Notes

Notes

Notes

~ Notes ~

Notes